Music

BARRON'S

Sounds and noises

Which are the five senses? Sight, touch, taste, smell, and …? This list is missing the sense we need to hear all the sounds around us. Surely you know which one it is: Hearing! You know it so well that you have been using it since you were very little, even when you were still inside your mom's belly. Do you remember what you could hear then?

Playful music

When you listen to music it seems that the sounds are all playing together. They get along so well that they make you feel different things: Sometimes you feel sad, but at other times the music is so happy you feel like jumping, dancing, and laughing. Music is like a magic language you can use to say many things without speaking any actual words.

However, to really enjoy music, you have to learn how to listen.

Two-count rest

Quarter-note rest

Whole rest

Silence (or rest)

Music is made of a combination of sounds and silence. Sometimes silence is very long, but at other times it is so short we don't even notice it. Without sounds and silence music would not exist.

But if you pay close attention, you will notice there is no complete and absolute silence anywhere. Try it: Go to the quietest place you know and listen carefully. Even covering your ears you can hear something, right?

A landscape of sounds

Close your eyes and listen … What do you hear? Just by the noise you can guess whether you are in a city, in the middle of the woods, or on the beach. You can even guess if it is day or night. It's as if you were watching a landscape, but instead of seeing things, you hear them.

Now, try to count how many sounds you can distinguish with your eyes closed.

Triangle

Cymbals

What intense sound!

Get a drumstick or any little stick and beat the table *verry* softly. Little by little, start beating a bit harder, but don't overdo it. It sounds different, doesn't it? It is the same sound, but the sensation we feel is different. You can do it with all the instruments you have at home.

There are many musical pieces in which you can notice how the musicians go from a soft sound to a louder one or the other way around. Why don't you look for one?

Zambomba

Tambourine

Xylophone

Wood block

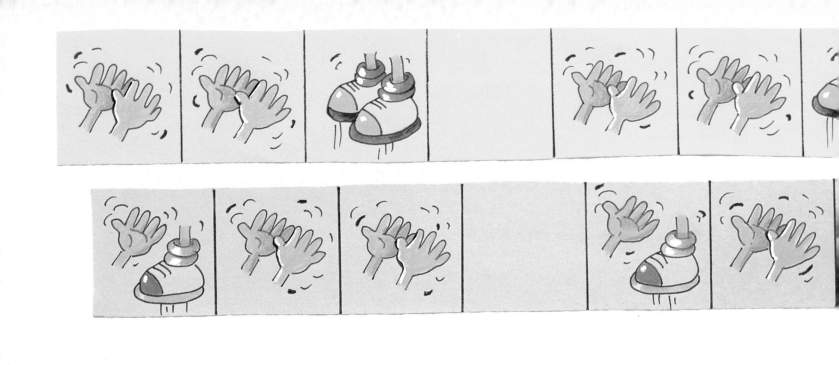

Follow the rhythm

Let's clap our hands! Clap, clap, clapclapclap, clap, clap, clapclapclap. We've just created a new rhythm! It's only a question of mixing sounds and silence of different lengths. Now try other rhythms and instruments. How about your feet?

A fast rhythm makes you clap your hands and stomp your feet when you hear music. When the rhythm is slow, you would rather listen to it sitting comfortably.

Let's make a song

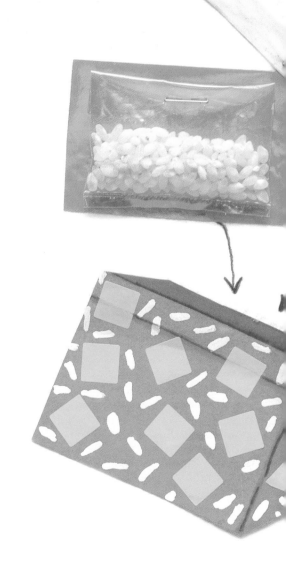

Now follow one of the rhythms you have invented with your foot and sing a song at the same time. Once you master the rhythm, you can use as many instruments as you wish: Pans, sticks, or bottles full of garbanzo beans. You'll get many different sounds this way!

To make it easier, you may follow the ticktock of a clock. Try inventing three different melodies with this rhythm.

15

Have you ever noticed that men and women have very different voices? A woman's voice is usually sharper, because the pitch is high. A man's voice, however, sounds deeper, with a low pitch.

High and low pitch

You can also make low-pitched sounds imitating the mooing of a cow or the moaning of a ghost, or high-pitched sounds imitating a newly hatched chick or the screeching brakes of a car. Do you have any suggestions?

Learning to write music

Music is written over lines. The deeper sounds are represented in the lower part and the sharper sounds in the higher lines. Each of these spots is called a musical note and they have names: C, D, E, F, G, A, B, or do (C), re (D), mi (E), fa (F), sol (G), la (A), si (B). In some countries they use only five notes instead of seven.

If you play these notes on a piano, it will seem like you are going up the stairs!

A musical voice

You can practice all the notes you already know with a musical instrument you always have with you, even when you go to bed. Can you guess which one it is? We're talking about your voice.

To start practicing, how about singing a song you know? Then sing it with your mouth shut, that is, without saying the words. And finally, sing it in front of a lit candle and try not to blow out the flame. Good luck.

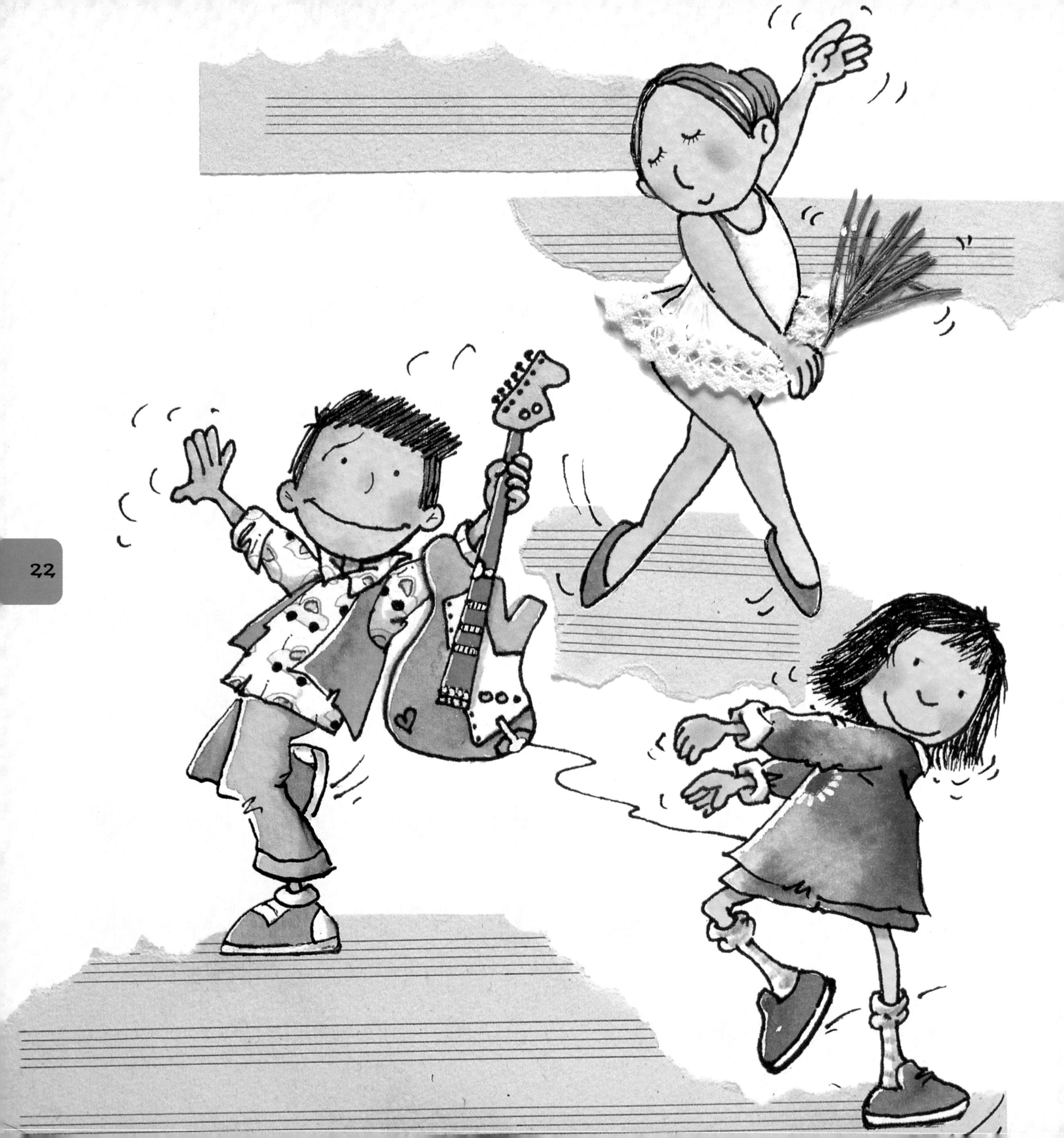

Shake your bones!

Dancing and music are twins. When you dance, you can express the music you feel inside of you even when you are not actually hearing it. Close your eyes and … can you hear music inside your body?

You can dance to music, you can make music with your voice, your hands, and your feet. Your body is a wonderful musical instrument.

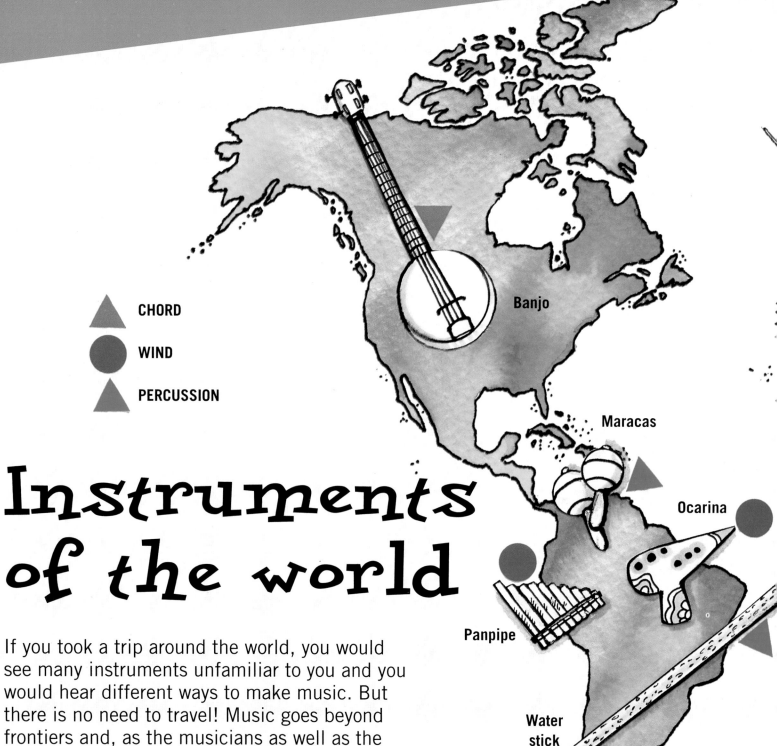

CHORD

WIND

PERCUSSION

Banjo

Maracas

Ocarina

Panpipe

Water stick

Instruments of the world

If you took a trip around the world, you would see many instruments unfamiliar to you and you would hear different ways to make music. But there is no need to travel! Music goes beyond frontiers and, as the musicians as well as the instruments travel all over, they get together and create new ways to make music.

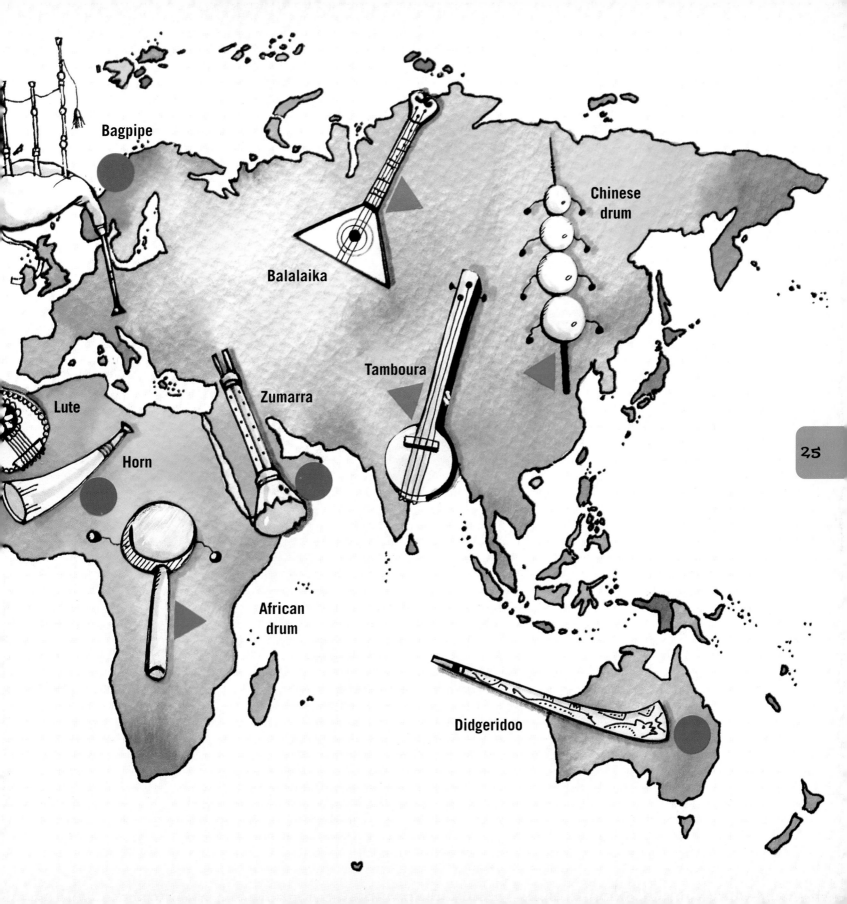

Bagpipe

Balalaika

Chinese drum

Lute

Zumarra

Tamboura

Horn

African drum

Didgeridoo

25

Music of the earth

If music is formed by sounds that go together, the earth is a great music composer: Water, wind, volcanoes, birds, crickets, and storms form an incredibly varied concert!

The music made by people will not always be pleasant to your ears. Some music will feel like noise and some other will simply not mean anything to you.

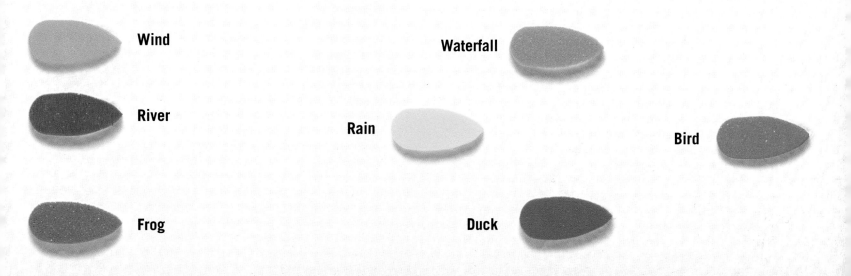

Wind

Waterfall

River

Rain

Bird

Frog

Duck

Music maestro!

Can you imagine a world without music? We do not need music to live, but with music our lives are much richer and more interesting. You can enjoy music by listening to it or playing it yourself, but if you want to know it well, first you must learn to hear everything around you.

Would you like to attend a music concert?

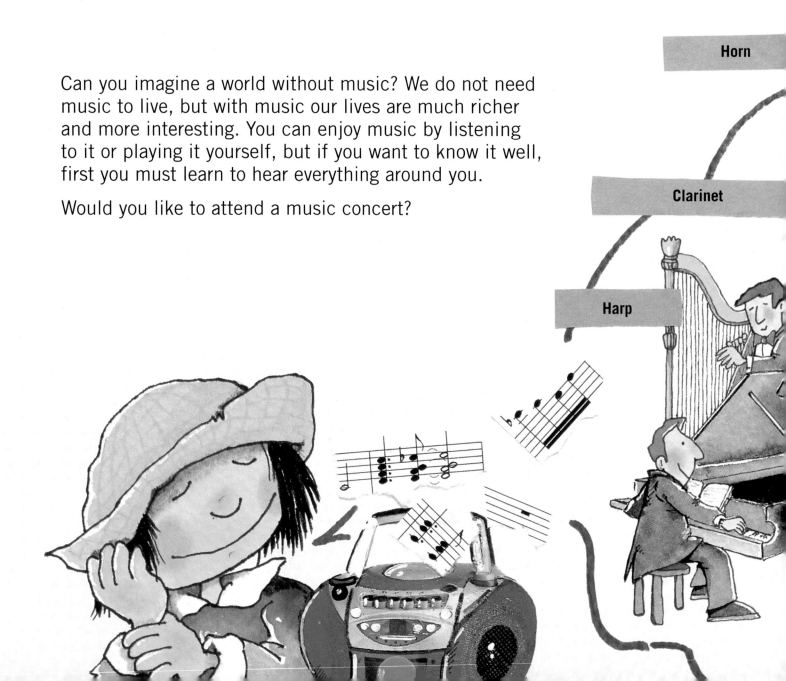

Horn

Clarinet

Harp

Activities

MAKE MARACAS!

To play with rhythm, we can make a musical instrument. For example, maracas. To make them, we need two yogurt containers and garbanzo beans.

1. Put the beans inside a clean yogurt container.
2. Glue the other container on top.
3. Decorate the maracas any way you wish and play! You can invent as many rhythms as you wish.

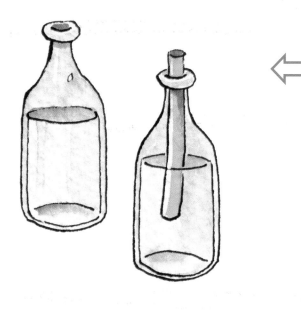

LOOKING FOR A MELODY

Not everyone agrees about what is music and what is not. Also, the way you make music depends on where in the world you live. But there is something we all agree on: The best way to understand music is to listen to it and to create it.

How about making music by following a melody? First we will make our instrument—a bottle piston.

1. Fill a bottle with water, about two-thirds full.
2. Cut a plastic tube about half an inch longer than the bottle. It can also be a piece of garden hose.
3. Introduce the tube into the bottle.

Now you can try the pitch of the sounds. If you raise or lower the tube while you blow, you will hear high- or low-pitched sounds.

Can you play or sing these melodic lines?

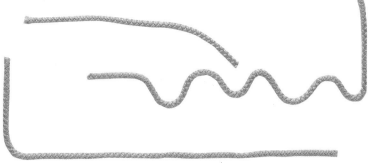

RHYTHM OF ANIMALS

How about imitating the sounds animals make?
Try to imitate each of the following rhythms.

Quarter note

Short sound
(one measure)

Half note

Longer sound
(two measures)

Whole note

Very long sound
(four measures)

kree kree kree kree kree kree kree kree

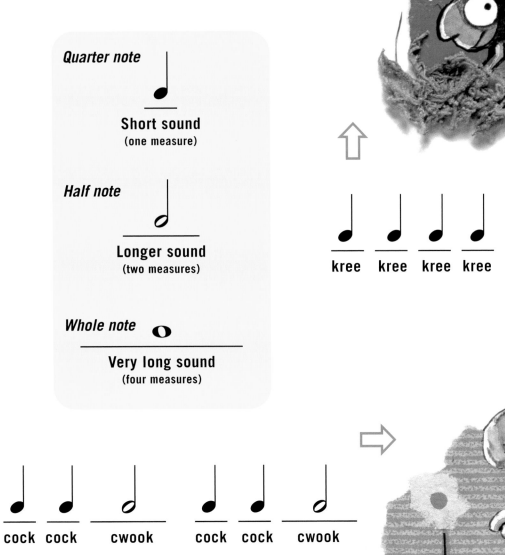

cock cock cwook   cock cock cwook

woof woof woof woof

moooooooooo

moooooooooo

Guide *to instruments*

MUSICAL INSTRUMENTS

String instruments produce sounds when you press or rub the strings. Here are a few from all over the world.

Harp

Violin

Sansa

Guitar

Saxophone

Accordion

Wind instruments make sounds when air goes through them.

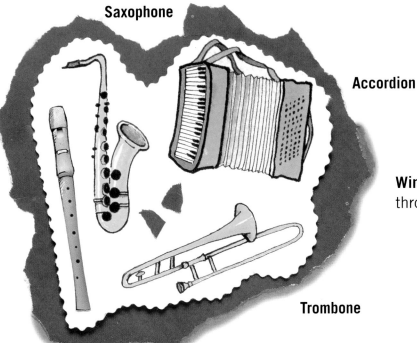

Trombone

Flute

Percussion instruments make sounds when they are struck.

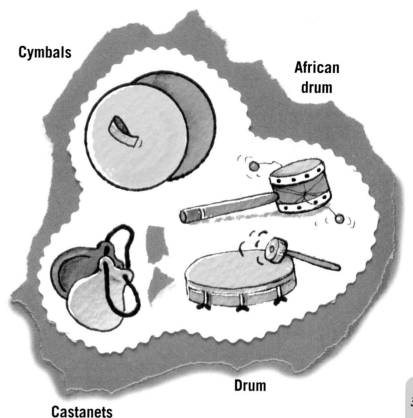

Cymbals

African drum

Drum

Castanets

Piano

Some are called **mixed instruments** because they combine features. Such is the case with the piano, which has **strings** that make sounds when they are **struck** by small hammers.

At present there are many instruments that run on electricity, such as those at right:

And new instruments continue to be invented!

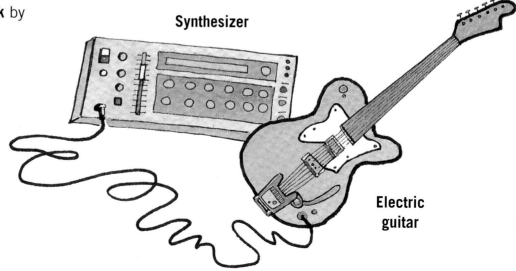

Synthesizer

Electric guitar